PAIN FORMATION

Forming Pain into Purpose

James Wilson

Editor: Rachel Arterberry

Cover Image: Lassedesignen/Shutterstock.com

Cover Design: 99designs

Printed in the United States of America

ISBN 978-0-578-49851-5

www.TheLifeofWilson.com

Table of Contents

FOREWORD

In my life, I have experienced many moments of pain. Unfortunately, your life may have many moments of pain. From my health issues to family issues, I should have failed at life years ago. However, I didn't. I trusted God and learned from my hurtful moments. You can trust God too. Pain can either break us or bring us closer to God. We get to choose to grow and transform our suffering into fulfilling God's purpose for our lives. Pain hurts you no matter your ethnicity, income level, education, or social status. The more painful experiences that occur in our lives, the more hurt we feel. We live through moments of doubt, frustration, and worry. The goal of this book is not to be a downer and tell you that life will never get better, so give up. Its purpose is quite the opposite. Life is precious, and we must fight for it.

Despite horrible situations that can drain our time, money, and energy, we must keep fighting. We have one life, so let's make it count!

I made this book short on purpose. I wanted to write a book that you could read in a day. Why? Because life is too short for you to waste your time. Pain can happen at any moment due to the unexpected phone call from a loved one or the sudden discomfort in your body. This book is short so you can finish it and apply it to your life. Finish the applications in the book. Read every chapter with an open heart to accept that God is in control and He loves you. May this book be a blessing to you. I hope my vulnerable moments of suffering encourage you to form your pain into purpose.

1. WHAT'S THE POINT?

Is there a point to all of our pain and suffering? I believe so. One of the most challenging things in life is to get past these situations. Some painful events are so grueling that they isolate you from other people and make you feel alone. We have to be careful with our feelings. Just because we think a certain way, does not make it accurate. There are times when you have to look back and become thankful for what you went through. The difference is that if you can make it through painful situations, you can help others. My goal isn't to tell you that life is the worst, you'll never get through it, and you should give up. It's like a football team. Each player practices relentlessly, most likely every day for hours out in the blazing sun, sweating, and probably smelling pretty severely. However, when game time comes, they are ready to get out on the field looking good and executing all the things that they've been practicing for hours.

In the same way, we need to be doing that with our lives. Although we know that there will be pain and struggles, we don't prepare. Since we don't prepare, we don't know what to do when the struggles come. Since we don't know what to do, we retreat and hide; we get angry and frustrated. Now, don't get me wrong. I am not saying that when things go badly, you should not get mad or frustrated. There are plenty of times when things went wrong for me. I was furious, frustrated, and wanted to be left all alone. Those feelings are normal and expected. However, the difference is that most people stay there and dwell on those feelings for years and decades without any relief.

In this book, I want to be vulnerable. I want to talk about some of the darkest times in my life and what I did in those difficult times during and after the pain. I am not sharing my story for personal glory. I want to share to help other people who are struggling daily to get through life. Let me say this, "You are not alone." I repeat, "You are not alone." You need to accept and believe this truth. Long after you read this book, things will pop up. People will become sick, bad things will happen, and you need to know what to do. The whole idea behind "Pain Formation" is to take a painful experience and form it into an empowering decision. Take control of your life. God is ultimately in control. He gives us control over what we do with the life that He's given us.

We are not robots. We have choices. Just as I carefully choose each word to put in this book, you also have options. There is not a microchip in my brain that is making me put each word on these pages. When bad things happen, we can choose to become bitter or better. As I've said before, I have decided to be bitter numerous times. As a matter of fact, I can't even count the times that I was bitter because of certain situations. However, throughout my life, I've learned to become better after painful things have occurred with the ultimate goal of helping others.

See, that's the thing. If you don't know what the goal is, then you're wasting your life. Imagine waking up in the morning, saying to yourself, "I don't know what I'm going to do today." Then you do that the next day. Then the next day and the next day. Do you get the point? I don't know of many people who wake up every day without a plan for their lives. If they don't have a plan for the day, they most likely don't have a job either. However, I am confident that's not you. You would not be reading this if you had not thought about some plan for your life; if you didn't believe that we can become stronger through unfortunate, dark, painful situations. I'm not trying to be all doom and gloom. The truth is, when we're hurting, we feel alone like nobody cares. We think that if it were someone else's problems rather than ours, we could keep moving forward. That's not the case. We have to live with the cards that we are dealt. Not to sound as if I don't care, but in reality, at the end of the day, when things go wrong, we need to know what to do. We need to know that we can transform pain into opportunities. We can serve other people and not just ourselves.

So, through this book, I invite you into my life, into the decisions that I made to help me get through the tough times. I want to offer you a chance to make a difference in someone else's life by making a decision. It's a difficult decision. Overall, it will be precious and necessary.

As you read about the things that I've been through, be careful not to disassociate yourself merely because it's not the specific issue that you have or may go through. A problem is a problem. Sure, you may solve problems differently than I do, but either way, problems must be solved. If your lightbulb goes out, you replace the bulb. If your phone's battery is going dead, you charge it. If you're feeling sick, you take medicine. If you're tired, you go to sleep. Different problems require different actions but remember they all must be solved. So, just because I share a problem that you've never been through, does not mean that you can't learn and grow from the solution in the process. Although you ultimately may solve your issue differently, you can still take the framework provided to you here and apply it to your own life.

I'm not looking for sadness. I'm not looking for a standing ovation. I'm not looking for a pat on the back. I'm looking for honesty. Ruthless honesty. Too often, in America, we see a "perfect" life. We see someone's life on Instagram, and it appears terrific. We see someone else's life on Facebook, and we see the best pictures with the best filters that no one else can even possibly replicate. Remember, we can't always believe what we see. We have to dig in deeper. We have to do some research, investigate, and analyze. Ask yourself the question, "Is this true?" When we do that, we take control of our lives. Don't believe everything that you see.

As I was slowly beginning to understand that there will be hiccups in my life, bumps, and bruises along the way, I realized that it does not mean that I can't learn from them and help others. My primary focus in this book will be health and family. Everyone has health. Everyone has a family. I am vague about these subjects now. Later, you'll see my motives for sharing these topics. I used "Pain Formation" by transforming my painful experiences into empowering decisions.

2. PAIN IN MY BODY

The Pain of a Rare Eye Disease

When I was in the third grade, everything seemed to fall apart. My mom and dad had divorced. Afterward, my mom, my sister, and I moved from Kannapolis, NC to Statesville, NC. I started noticing that I was having difficulty with my vision. Slowly, my vision became worse, and I was confused about what was going on. Even though I had glasses, my vision was becoming worse, and my left eye started to drift to the left. For years, I went to the eye doctor, and we would follow the same old routine; they would do a scan, examine my eyes, and get "results." Even after lengthy procedures, answers were varied and in fact, not really answers at all. Throughout elementary school, I did not just sit at the front of the row to see; I would have to get a copy of what was put on the board so that I could write it down on my paper. When I entered middle school, the same thing happened. I would get very close to the board to make sure I could see. It was difficult for anyone not to notice me. I was the kid sitting on the floor by the overhead projector. It's sad if you don't know what an overhead is because you'll never know the struggle. In reality, that shows how old I am. I had to be close to the overhead writing down my notes because I couldn't see it from anywhere else.

Afterward, I would go back to my seat, struggling with my confidence because everyone had watched me. I was just the kid who would raise his hand and ask if he could move closer. I used to hate it when the teacher would say, "James, you're already pretty close." How embarrassing! At the same time, I knew that if I didn't write things down, I would not be able to do the work. I did that for three years, all the way through middle school. I was lonely and afraid. I didn't know of anyone dealing with the same issues as me. I felt isolated and unloved. I didn't have my father to teach me about confidence. I became a scared little boy on the inside. I was broken and sad.

When I got in high school, my vision took a horrible turn, as if it could get any worse. Several times I even went blind. At some time during my childhood, my left eye had a retinal detachment, leaving me only to be able to see out of my right eye. I could only vaguely make out faint colors with my left eye. Here I was, a high schooler, walking around not looking at people in the eye because I had such low self-esteem and confidence in myself. One of the most challenging things for me was always feeling like I was alone and that no one was going through what I was. I always saw couples hugging each other and holding hands. I thought no one would love me because I was ugly. No one will love me because of my eyes. No one would love me because of my bad eyesight. I was sad, depressed, and did not like myself.

I often looked in the mirror. Was I thankful for my eyesight? Absolutely. At the same time, from the outside, my life seemed pretty good. People told me regularly that I was funny, and I had good jokes. However, internally, I was broken. I was alone. I was hurting and crying out to God to stop my pain. I didn't like who I was. I was upset at God because He made me this way. I couldn't understand why God would do this to my eyes, knowing that I would go through so much pain. I have prayed for healing over and over and over and over and over and over and over, but it never came.

I'll share the most recent time I lost my vision. In 2015, I woke up around 5:00 am and went to the gym. I ran on the treadmill and lifted some weights. I was feeling pretty good, so I went over to the bench press machine. I did some heavy lifting that strained my muscles. I finished up my workout, went home, and got ready for church. When Alison and I arrived at the church, I noticed the car seemed brighter than usual. Unfortunately, the brightness of the vehicle was reflecting off of the fluid filling my eye. I immediately knew what was about to happen because this had happened several times before. I had roughly 30 minutes before I lost my eyesight.

We immediately drove to the nearest eye doctor and waited. When we finally got a chance to see the doctor, he seemed as shocked as I was as to what he saw. He even told us that he wasn't qualified to help. Right there on the spot, he called his colleague and professor at UAB Callahan Eye Hospital and shared everything he saw in my eye. The next thing we knew, Alison and I were on a 3-hour trip to Birmingham, AL. It seemed like hours of waiting and exams. I'm so thankful for a wonderful wife to be there by my side. After what seemed like forever, the doctor told me everything I needed to know. You see, ever since I started having problems with my eyes, I've been told this and that. I have been misdiagnosed tons of times. However, that day in Alabama, I was finally given answers.

I have Wagner's (Vagner's) Syndrome. It's a rare hereditary eye disease. So unique that there are only a couple hundred known cases. My connective tissues, also called collagen, are weak. Any strong vibration, such as straining my muscles, heavy lifting, running, hammering, riding roller coasters, you name it, will cause my retina to pull which opens up my eye for fluid to fill it, causing me not to be able to see. The fluid usually takes weeks to drain, but I didn't care. I was sitting in the chair listening to the doctor, and although I couldn't see his face, I was so thankful for an answer about my eyes.

Sometimes, unfortunately, we put our struggles in front of someone else's. It is hard to think of other people when we are in pain. I don't know about you, but if I ever stub my toe, I am seldom thinking of someone else stubbing theirs. My pain is more important to me than any pain that anyone else is going through at that moment. It's hard not to be selfish or self-focused when we're going through agony and times of struggle. If I told you that I thought of other people during my battle with my eyes initially, that would be a lie. The only person I thought of was myself. I'm sure you've done that as well.

Just because we think of ourselves when we're hurting, doesn't mean we're bad people. It just means we're trying to get through the pain to feel better. For me, when dealing with my eyes, year after year, it felt like better was never coming. Have you ever felt that "better" was never coming for you, your health, or your family? Me too. It is hard not to lose faith when you don't see anything changing. Just because things are not changing does not mean that

God's not moving in our lives. Just because we don't see the engine under the hood, does not mean that the car is not operating correctly. Sure, we can hear the engine. Sure, we can feel the vibrations from the engine. Hearing and feeling the engine is seldom different than seeing it.

Let's say you're walking on the sidewalk. You begin to hear and feel the vibrations of a car. You can sense it's getting closer and closer to you. You wouldn't just stop and look at that car driving off the road towards you and keep walking. You're going to be looking for that car as fast as you can to ensure that you get out of the way to safety. When things aren't going so well, people try to help by saying helpful things and offering support. Some people give you hugs while others cry with you, but it's still difficult when you don't see the change. It's even harder when you're having problems with your vision, and you don't see that God is moving.

The Pain of Psoriasis

I remember when I was a young boy, getting up and doing my morning routine; wake up, put some lotion on my face, and go to school. I put the cream on my face because it would get so dry that my skin would peel throughout the day. No matter what I tried, my skin would dry up and peel. During class, I'd try to go to the bathroom to wash my face with water. Unfortunately, the water would dry up and make my skin dry again. Imagine how I felt whenever I knew that my face was peeling. Talk about low self-worth. I went through elementary and middle school, avoiding to look at people eye to eye. As I entered high school, my skin stayed dry. However, something different started to happen. I began getting scars on my wrist. Curious about what was happening, I went to a dermatologist, and they told me that I had ringworms. So, I got cream and put it on my body every day; nothing changed. Each week, I would put more cream on the scars on my arms, but then more scars began to pop up. They started to appear all over my body; on my arms, on my legs, on my back...all over. As an adult, I learned that I have psoriasis.

Psoriasis is basically when your body thinks that you have a cut and so it makes a scab over clean skin instead of an actual wound. There are scabs all over my body, but under the scabs is clean skin. Stress is a significant factor with psoriasis. Whenever I'm stressed, my psoriasis kicks in and starts creating scabs all over my arms and my body. Of course, I was very self-conscious about myself and my body since I was getting scabs all over me; my psoriasis was causing my psoriasis!

I didn't know what to do. I didn't know what to put on it because it was confusing why it was happening. 'Why was it happening to me?' That was the question I was asking. Have you ever asked that question? I think we've all asked it. There's nothing wrong with asking, "Why is this happening to me." There is something wrong in saying, "That this cannot happen to me." We are not promised health. We are not promised another day of life. We are not promised $1 million with the mansion and seven cars. We are promised with the love of God; we are promised, through our faith in Christ, to spend eternity with our heavenly father who loves us. It's challenging to love yourself when you don't like yourself.

I was having a tough time with my skin and in fact, loving my skin. I would wear a long-sleeve shirt and jeans, layering up so no one would be able to tell what was going on with my skin. I was suffering. I was in pain. I was dealing with the blow of hiding who I was because it wasn't "normal." Throughout the years, I was able to love myself and learn how to love myself. I learned how to look at myself in the mirror and truly be thankful for who God created me to be. As I said, this is throughout the years and not throughout the day. This took a long time.

Transforming painful situations into purpose is not merely a snap of the fingers. I wish it were, but it's not. It's almost like you're jogging down the street or you're exercising, and your body gets tired. All you want to do is give up and say, "Well, I'm tired. That's it! I'm going to go home, eat a bag of chips, and ice cream because I worked out." Instead, you push through the pain because you know the reward is greater than the actual suffering. Not to say that suffering is not real. Suffering hurts very much. On the other hand, you exercise or jog through the pain because you know you can reach the goal of being healthy and losing weight.

The same can be said for transforming pain into empowerment. First, you look at the pain. Feel the pain. You share the pain with others. You examine the pain. Share the heavy load with loved ones because they care for you. You can't be in denial. We live in a culture where everyone says they're okay with a big rod through their stomach. We cannot be in denial and smile in other people's faces saying, "Everything is OK." No one expects you to be perfect. If they do, get away from them. The only person who is perfect and will always be perfect is Jesus Christ himself, and that does not include you or me. The reason why it's so crucial for us to know that we are in pain and that the pain is real is that we can give that pain to Christ. We are not called to carry our pain all alone and deal with it all by ourselves. Unfortunately, we try to be the hero of our story.

Know that Christ has shed His blood in pain for you! We smile and wave, showing big white teeth, nodding our heads, pretending that we're 10 out of 10. Stop doing it. Stop acting like you are the greatest thing ever to happen. Stop pretending that you know all the answers. We're not called to do that. Do not accept the lie that you have to be perfect. I can tell you one thing. I'm not perfect. I am a hot mess! I am so thankful for the wife that God has blessed me with because I need help. I forget where I put my keys. I forget to drink water and then I get a headache because I'm dehydrated.

Sometimes, I forget where I put my wallet for eight days out of the week. Yes, you read that correctly. Eight days out of the week is how many times I lose my wallet. That's precisely what I'm talking about. There are so many things that I am not good at. I need help. Thank the Lord that Alison helps me. Did I mention that I'm a hot mess? The reason why I'm sharing this is to let you know that I know that I'm not perfect. I'm an author. So what? I'm not perfect. I'm a pastor, but I'm not perfect. I may have a large social media following, but I'm not perfect. When we realize that we don't have to have it all together, it leaves room for you and me to ask Jesus for help.

It's almost like a child who is struggling to put on their shoes or open the door. You and I don't just watch them and laugh while we're waiting for them to ask you for help because you know you can solve the problem. We're like that kid. We're trying to put our shoes on all by ourselves, and we have no idea which foot goes where. We're trying to put our hands in the shoes and the shoestrings in our mouths. We have no idea what's going on, but we try over and over to fix our problems. At the same time, God is waiting on us to reach out to Him to help us carry the load that we shouldn't be taking on our own.

The only way we can take a painful situation and transform it into a purpose is to let God do what only He can do. God's perspective is a whole lot better than mine. When I see things, I first see them the way I want too, and I feel the way I want too, and then I do it the way I want too. This certainly is not the best choice. Usually, it ends with pain, anger, frustration, or just giving up. Instead, I need to say, "God, I don't understand what's happening. God, help me to trust you in this time of need. God, give me your strength because I need you." It's also about relying on loved ones and speaking to them. I know it's weird to tell people that you need help and that you need love and that everything is not ok. People respect you when you share things with them. Why? They get to see you handle certain situations that inspire and encourage them. Being honest makes them reflect on their own lives and ways of handling difficult situations.

So, let's go back to my skin. As I'm writing this book, I have psoriasis scars all over my elbows and shins. My ears peel because of psoriasis. Every morning, after I take a shower, I moisturize my face with Aquaphor. I put it on my arms, face, and ears every single day. However, throughout the day, the moisture starts to wear off, and my body begins to dry up again. So, I apply it again. There's also an essential factor associated with my process. I have done something special. I have taken the pain from psoriasis and transformed it into a purpose in my life.

My appearance does not define me. God knew me before I was ever born. God knew that I would have psoriasis and struggle with it my whole life. God also knew that as I grew, I would trust Him with my skin. I know that God accepts me for who I am. I trust God and know that my skin doesn't stop me from being a better husband, a better father, or a better Christ-follower. The doubts caused by my skin condition put a gap between God and me. I had to take my faith and place it in between that gap of doubt. When I placed faith in the hole, I made the empowering decision of trusting God that He knew what He was doing and that He knows what's best for me.

I've been able to help people who have been struggling with their appearance to have confidence in themselves. I can wear shorts with confidence even though my legs have scars on them. I can go to the beach without a shirt even though I have scars all over my chest and my back. I can walk in a room with a short sleeve shirt on even though I have scars from psoriasis on my elbows. No matter my "blemishes," Christ died for me, and that's something to walk in with bold faith. I want you to understand that Christ died for you as well. Any pain that you are going through, with your physical appearance or with your health or maybe with a particular situation, know that God knew that you would go through it before you ever did. Know that it's OK that you're not OK. But you can't stay there. Reach out to God and place faith in the gap between you and God. Ask Christ to carry your load instead of you taking it. When you do this, you get God's perspective, and then that's when you will be blessed in learning from the pain and transforming it into purpose.

I used to struggle with my skin. Now, I completely own it. I smile about it. I get to share about it boldly to encourage and inspire others. Honestly, I can't think of a time when I was afraid or ashamed of who God called me to be. And remember, it has nothing to do with my power. It's all because I know that it's not my power at all, but through God's power and me trusting Him.

Application

When you look in the mirror, who do you see?

What do you think about yourself?

Who is someone you can be honest with and tell them when you're not ok?

Why do you think people are so afraid to let others know of their pain?

Why do you think God allowed you to go through what you have gone through?

Share your answers on social media using the hashtag "#PainFormation"

3. UNEXPECTED PAIN ON VACATION

The biggest thing about health is that everyone has it. Sure, yours can be better than someone else's. You can be a little healthier in how you eat, your habits, and your routines, but we all have health. Some may have to monitor their health more than others. Some can eat whatever they want without gaining a pound. I wish that were me. All I would do is eat cinnamon rolls and honey buns. Unfortunately, I would gain 5 pounds per bite of pastries. Seriously! The thing about our health is that when things are good, we are good. But when things are bad, our whole life shifts upside down.

Back in 2017, Alison and I went to an extraordinary place for our fifth anniversary. We planned to go to Florida to go to Universal Studios and Disney. While we were gone, my mom had agreed to come down to Mississippi to watch our son Eli. Can you say free childcare? So, we go on this journey, spending time together, holding hands and frolicking in the wind. We go to Universal Studios, and we are having a blast; eating amazing food and buying things that we didn't need. We were enjoying every last minute of our time together. I mean, who cares when you're on vacation, right!

Everything was great. Just think of a movie about a couple spending time together with smiles and genuinely enjoying each other's time. That was us. Everything was great until we got to Disney. We upgraded our passes, and then we went to Epcot for the Food and Wine Festival. Now, if you've never been to Disney for the Food and Wine Festival, what are you doing with your life? Seriously, go. I'm not getting paid to say that, but I am saying that you are missing out. When you get there, you receive a booklet that has a ton of different countries where you can try their food. So, Alison and I opened up our brochure and decided to start in China.

As we walked around the entire lake, we ate food from every country available. We ate so much........ I can't even remember. Just food and food and food. When we got to France, I had the crème brûlée. Little did I know, I was about to witness pain. While I was eating the crème brûlée, I started feeling weird. It was the kind of weird when you don't feel normal, but you can't figure out what's going on. That kind of weird. I was feeling this heaviness in my stomach and my chest. I wasn't sure what was happening. Honestly, I just thought my stomach was too full. So, Alison asked me, "Are you OK?" I replied, "I don't feel so good."

At this time, Alison was still breastfeeding our son, so she still had to pump milk even though Eli was hours away with my mother in Mississippi. She had to go to the nursing station. May I remind you, while on our way to the nursing station, I still was not feeling well. However, I happened to notice Hawaii, which had a gleaming sign from Heaven that read, "Hawaiian Cheesecake."

Let's pause here because I know what you're saying. Don't judge me. We all make mistakes. Let's say I made a poor choice. Ok, let's get back on track. I felt like cheesecake angels had hovered over the sign, singing, "James, eat me even though you're not feeling well. It's OK. God will forgive you. All will be better. Eat me." I knew I wasn't feeling well. I knew that if I took one more bite, I might explode, literally. But you know what? I did it. I went to the stand and asked for one slice of Hawaiian cheesecake. I was gasping and wheezing, not feeling well at all. I was close to what felt like death, but I still wanted to eat one last bite. If I'm going to die at Disney, I'm going out with a piece of Cheesecake and greeting my Father in Heaven! When I got the cheesecake, I hunched over and could barely breathe. I was so ill that I could barely talk and yet I was trying to stuff this soft and creamy, delicious Hawaiian cheesecake in my mouth. Alison was waiting for me because we had to walk to the nursing station. Remember, I could barely walk at this point, but yet I was still trying to be greedy.

As I slowly made it to the nursing station, I was so full and felt so badly about having to throw away the costly ($8) small, thin-sliced piece of delicious Hawaiian cheesecake. I didn't know what was going on. I felt horrible. I laid down on some chairs and asked the nurse there if I could have some medicine to help me feel better. She showed her concern for me, asking if I was OK and getting me a cup of water. I asked her where the first aid station is because I was not feeling well at all. She told me it was next-door. So, while Alison was pumping breast milk, I went over to the first aid station, about to pass out. They put me on a bed, started asking me tons of questions, and checking my blood pressure. Gasping for air, I knew that something was wrong, I didn't know what. The kind workers decided to call the ambulance.

Have you ever seen an ambulance roll through the beautiful land of Epcot? Me neither. I was inside the first aid station, moaning in pain, so I'm not sure what it looked like from the onlookers. What I do know is that as I got on the stretcher, everyone working in the first aid station at Disney, conveniently left their stations to stand out in the hallway to watch me get an IV strapped in and then rolled out. Let's say it was worse than embarrassing. When I finally got to the ER, they began running a ton of tests. Alison and I sat there, pretty much freaking out. Our flight back home was scheduled for the next day, and it was looking like we were not leaving. The nurse informed me that after many tests, they determined that I had gallstones. If you have never experienced gallstones, let's say it's close to being shot in the stomach and then someone is trying to rip the bullet out by hand.

Although the doctors were saying that I needed to have surgery immediately, I was telling them that our plane was going to leave the next day and we needed to go with it back home to Mississippi. I asked for some medication to allow me to handle the pain until I got back home where I could have surgery. All was well. I was able to get back home, take some meds, and have surgery. Now, be glad you didn't spend a ton of money for your 5th anniversary and end up owing a ton of money during your 5th anniversary. It's like we left Mississippi spending a ton of money and we left Florida owing a ton of money. So, in the end, when you're celebrating your anniversary, don't go to Florida and don't get the Hawaiian cheesecake.

So, what was the lesson learned in this terrible experience?

I learned that you could save up all the money you want to go on that perfect trip that you planned in your head. You know the one. The journey in the movies where they go to the ideal place with the ideal weather and the perfect food and everything is just perfect with the perfect music? That one. Yeah, that doesn't happen. But what does happen? A relationship strengthened through tough times. Throughout that whole time, my wife never complained; she didn't complain about how much money we were going to owe, about how hot it was, about how tired she was, or anything like that. The only thing that Alison did was comfort me, care for me, and love me. During that time of pain, I was always moaning and hurting. But my loving wife didn't complain and cared for me the entire time.

I learned through that whole situation that I could change my terrible experience into a purpose. I could form something useful from this pain. I could take the appalling experience of gallstones and transform it into an empowering choice that says and claims with boldness: I will love my spouse. That's it. I will love my spouse. Too often, we argue and fuss over the stupid little things that pull us entirely apart. But one thing to remember is that love is a choice. If somebody is forcing you to love them, then that is not love. We freely choose to love someone or not love them. We freely choose to be focused on the small part of a specific situation that can completely ruin an entire relationship. As I was sitting there in pain, I could see the look on my wife's face. I could see that she cared for me. I could see that she loved me. I could look back and think of all the stupid conversations there were; the silly conversations that made us so upset and annoyed at each other. The only thing that mattered was me and my health. See that's the thing when our health goes towards a downward spiral, our mind opens up to what's essential. We start seeing things for what they are.

When you're sick, you're not trying to purchase a mansion and buy 40 cars and the latest cell phone. When you're sick, you want to be loved. You want to be cared for. You want to feel a sense of belonging. So, what can you and I do before our health goes to a downward spiral? We must choose to love the people around us. Choosing to love them will help us for when we get better or when we're healthy to truly not let the small things get in the way. It's because I choose to love my wife that I don't mind her turning the ceiling fan on at night. Side note: I hate the ceiling fan. I hate being cold and I hate the ceiling fan on because it makes me cold. But because I choose to love my wife freely, I will have that ceiling fan blast on the fastest setting because the woman I love lays beside me.

Forming pain into purpose isn't rocket science. It's about taking an experience and choosing the life that you want to live. But to choose, you have to decide. You can select something that's not empowering. For example, I'm just going to take my health for granted, and I'm going to love no one and be completely selfish. Good luck finding anyone to love you back. Nobody wants to be around anyone like that. An empowering decision is about loving somebody because you choose too. When you choose to love, you see what's important.

In this life, there are a ton of distractions. There are commercials and ads everywhere. They are even on your social media. They're everywhere! So, when we experience an immediate drop in our health, only then do we bypass the ads to what really matters. In that moment of pain, the only thing that mattered to me was my family. It's humbling how pain and suffering can help us focus on what truly matters on this earth with the short amount of time that we have. No one is promised tomorrow. So how much longer are you going to keep allowing pain to shape how you view and approach life?

Application

Think about your past or current painful situations.

What have you learned about yourself?

What have you learned about others?

When you had something terrible happen to you, what was your initial reaction?

Is it the same thought today?

Think of one thing you can do today to prepare yourself for a difficult season in life.

Share your answers on social media using the hashtag "#PainFormation"

4. THE PAIN OF AN ABSENT FATHER

As I said earlier, my parents divorced when I was in 3rd Grade. At the time, we lived in Kannapolis, NC. If you haven't heard about it, then don't worry because it's a small town. After the divorce, my mom, sister, and I moved to Statesville, NC, another small town. We moved into a quiet trailer park in a single-wide trailer. We all had our own room. From 3rd grade until I graduated High School, I vaguely remember my father being in my life because there are no memories of just us doing something together. Growing up without a father was agony. It was painful and full of suffering. Days would go by, and I would wonder what was wrong with me and why my dad didn't want any part of me. Birthdays, Holidays, sports games, band competitions, and more all went by without my dad being there. Years of hearing my friends talk about their parents poured salt on the open wound that was burning my soul like acid. I remember telling my mom 'Happy Father's Day' one year, and I've done it ever since. Growing up without a father taught me several valuable lessons.

First, let me reiterate that the pain is genuine, and the feeling of abandonment comes at a cost. I've seen it over and over before when young boys growing up without a dad make terrible, life-altering choices, the type of decisions that end them up in jail, on drugs, or worse, dead. For me, not having my dad around was embarrassing and shameful. But year after year, through every event, every memory, every accomplishment, my desire for my father's approval slowly died. I wasn't in band class to seek my dad's consent. I didn't play football, basketball, rugby, tennis, marching band, drums, trumpets, quads, or any other activity in school for his approval. And yes, I did all of those things. My mother worked very hard to support my sister and me. She worked 12 hours a day for years. When we would come home from school, my mother would leave to go to work. I don't know how she did it, but she always took care of us. She placed her wants behind ours.

Every year, we had a fantastic Christmas. We had birthdays and movie nights. Almost every Friday, my mom would take my sister, Shavonne, and I to the video store for each of us to pick a movie. Afterward, we'd head to the grocery store to get a snack. I remember those days like it was yesterday. I vividly remember picking out the horror movie "The Ring" and getting a pack of sugar cookies and milk. I watched that movie and was scared to death. I barely slept that night. Sure, we lived in a trailer park, but I had one of the best childhoods a child could ever have. I can't imagine how on Earth a single mom can raise two children, with one income. It truly baffles me. It's incomprehensible. Honestly, the more I think about my childhood, the easier it was for me to transform my pain from the abandonment of my father to the loving arms of my mother.

Once again, the pain is very real. Now, as a man, I still have to deal with the painful past I endured. I reflect on what could have and should have happened. I think about how different my life would be "if." I look at my son, Eli, and smile because I'm so thankful God trusts me to be a father. When I get discouraged, I think about the amazing memories of my childhood and how God provided me with a loving mom who helped me grow into a man. I remember when my mom had "the talk" with me. We were pulling into the trailer park, and she began telling me how I could talk to her about anything. And the rest of the conversation was me trying to jump out of the car, hoping to get run over instead of hearing my mom talk to me about sex. But I look at that moment and see a woman of bravery and courage. I see a parent who played the cards she was dealt. And because of her doing so, I was able to grow and replicate that same care to my child. Eli may never know who his grandfather is, but he will know that his daddy loves him. I transformed that pain from my dad into purpose by saying, "God will always provide for me."

As a child, I prayed that God would get my parents back together. Did that happen? No. Did God answer my prayer in the way I wanted? No. However, God answered my prayer according to His perfect will. I grew up with my mom and sister right until I got into high school, and that's when God answered my prayer in a way I never expected.

You see, I believe that God doesn't waste hurt. Some things in life don't feel good. God sees it and knows it. When I was young, I got into skateboarding. It was an escape for me. It was the only thing that I could do where I could be alone. I put energy into every trick. I'd fall sometimes. I would land the trick other times. Nevertheless, hard work helped me to feel accomplished. I would skateboard for hours and hours. I would be gone on Saturdays from sunup to sundown skateboarding. It was a mental Utopia. When I was skateboarding, I wasn't thinking about my father, my eyes, or any concern. I was only thinking about landing the trick. So, I would go out on an adventure and come home sweaty and tired. I started skateboarding in Statesville, NC and continued even when we moved to Charlotte, NC.

I remember it as if it were yesterday. I was skateboarding in a church parking lot because I didn't want to be home and while I was there, a white van pulled up. I'm not kidding. A white van. I was all alone. In a parking lot. Sounds creepy? Praise the Lord it was the youth pastor and a group of boys with skateboards coming out of the van. They had just left the skate park in Charlotte and got back to the church. I didn't go to that church. I was just some punk kid on private property skateboarding. The guy came out, looked at me and said, "You can't skateboard here." My mother didn't raise me to be disrespectful to adults, so I said, "Yes sir." I was about to be on my way when he asked me a question, the question that no man has ever asked me before. "What are you doing this Sunday? Do you want to come to church?" It was such a silly question, yet, so powerful.

There I was, in a parking lot, running away from my home life, searching for something and God met me where I was. I replied that I wasn't doing anything that Sunday and I'd come to church. I went to church as a kid. However, with my mother working so much, we didn't attend frequently. She did her best and exposed me to church, and for that I'm grateful.

I began attending the church and got plugged into the youth group. I was the usual class clown. At the same time, I was all in! I basically lived at that church. I'd visit my youth pastor pretty frequently to hang out. That same youth pastor I met in a parking lot when I was around 16, is the same pastor and dear friend who led me to Christ, baptized me, guided my girlfriend to Christ, baptized my girlfriend, led my premarital counseling, officiated my wedding, and so much more. God's grace is sufficient. We must have faith and lean into painful situations because God will not waste the hurt. Stephen has been a father to me for a long time. I'm thankful he took me in and cared for me. Some lessons he taught me helped me grow into the husband, father, and pastor that I am today.

Sometimes, God does provide for you and me in the most unlikely ways. Stephen is a white man. I'm a black man. With us, we embrace our differences and love each other as brothers. God provided someone for me in place of the void of acceptance by my father. I am so thankful God answered my prayers even better than I could imagine. We tend to expect God to answer our prayers in our way. God's ways are higher than ours so, by all means, let God do His thing.

Now that I'm a father, I look at life from a different perspective. My son, Eli, is two years old right now. Just this morning, when he saw me, he ran up to me with outstretched arms and said, "Daddy!" Being a parent is a privilege. I desire to teach Eli the ways of the Lord and to live them out for him to see. Growing up without a father does put a fire inside of me for Eli. I want to be there for him when he needs me. I know what it's like to play sports, go to band competitions, and other experiences without your dad there. Eli won't know what that is like. God willing, I'll be right there screaming his name! I'll be screaming any other names of our future kids too!

Now and then, fear creeps up within me. I start thinking that I didn't grow up with my dad, so I'm unqualified to be a father. Michael Hyatt calls this thinking "Limited Beliefs." He's right! This statement limits my potential as a parent because of my past. I do not believe in that thinking. So, when it tries to sneak in my mind, I say, "God has provided for me." I then recall all of the uncomfortable conversations I had with Stephen to deal with my rejection, sadness, and anger about my dad.

One day, the conversation went from listening to being angry. I was in Stephen's office, expressing my frustration for my dad. I was trying to figure out "why" he just wasn't there. Stephen sat back in his chair and listened patiently like he always did. Once I finished, he opened a drawer from his desk, pulled out a piece of paper, closed the drawer, and leaned forward. I thought he was about to write something mesmerizing down, something life-changing and wise like Solomon or Socrates. However, that's not what happened at all. He held that piece of paper and said,

"James, think of this full sheet of paper as who you want your dad to be." I was like, "ok?" Then, he ripped a corner of the full sheet. He held the rest of the paper with a ripped edge and said, "But this is who your dad is. You want him to be a full sheet of paper, but he's not. He never will be."

I sat back in my chair, stunned, confused, and disappointed. I thought for a moment and said, "Well, why doesn't my dad just become a full sheet of paper and just be a part of my life?" Stephen, holding up the paper with a ripped corner, said, "Because this is your dad." Again, I sat back becoming angrier. For the life of me, I couldn't understand the "ripped" corner. To me, it's such an easy fix. I'm your son, and you're my dad, so fix the "brokenness" and be in my life. Frustrated, I told Stephen, "Why can't he just fix the corner?"

Stephen held up the paper again and said that's my father. We went back and forth and back and forth. He merely kept repeating himself until it finally happened. It sank in. For the first time in my life, I gained clarity on the hurt, pain, sadness, and anger I had been dealing with for years. I was forcing myself to try and make someone become what I want them to be. I realized that I couldn't change anyone, but I can change myself. Ripped sheet or not, it's not my responsibility to "fix" people. However, it is my responsibility for how I respond.

It's your responsibility for how you respond as well. You can't change anyone. However, you can deal with the emotions and move on from there. Take it one day at a time whenever those feelings start to rise. Remember, we can't expect people to be who we want them to be. Sometimes, we must move on and unfortunately leave others behind who don't want to be a part of our journey. If someone wants to go on a long road trip and invites me, I'll kindly pass on that offer. So why do we try to "force" people to go on our journey of life with us? It's almost like kidnapping or a hostage situation. If someone clearly doesn't want to be in your life, let them go. God provides. I can speak that with bold confidence because God has done it for me. I'm thankful for my father. Without him, I wouldn't be born from my current family. I am grateful for Stephen. I pray for him often. I want to do the same thing for another young man that was done for me.

Application

Who are you forcing to be a part of your life?

Why are you trying to force them?

What is one step you can make to let them go?

How would your life look like if you stopped trying to force people in your life?

Know that God does provide according to His will, not yours. You must endure painful situations to help someone else who is in need.

Share your answers on social media using the hashtag "#PainFormation"

5. DON'T GET CRUSHED

Pain is real! If anyone says differently, you may want to distance yourself away from them. I haven't met a single person being punched in the face who said, "Mhhh, I don't feel anything." Our goal isn't to pretend as if the pain from any situation is not there. It is not good to suppress your emotions. If you do, they will eventually come out at a later time. Believe me, living with my eye disease is harder than I can say. Each day of my life, I try to be as careful as possible not to do anything that could jeopardize my vision. At the same time, I remember that the next day is not even guaranteed for me to be alive. So, I must live each day as if it were my last. That doesn't mean I go out partying and spending all my money on expensive things.

For me, it's more of a personal reflection of what did I do with the responsibilities that God gave me. Right now, I'm writing this book with my two-year-old son in the same room. It's 7:20 am on Tuesday. My wife is off today because of an appointment later. She is sleeping in. I'm more focused on how I am showing my wife love today and disciplining my family. So, my daily decisions are based on keeping the end in mind.

If we are not careful, our pain can crush us, even to the point of depression or even suicide. In my lowest and most hurtful moments, there is a pattern that keeps coming up. I've always asked for help. Did you know that Satan is a master of tricks? His whole purpose is to seek, kill, and destroy. Lies can feel very real. We have to be careful not to trust our feelings during stressful situations. Another big lie is that you have to be alone to handle suffering because nobody cares. Now, being detached to process and feel is not a bad thing. It is terrible to withdraw so much to where people can't get ahold of you. You're not picking up your phone or not responding to people reaching out to you. I understand how it feels. During the times I lost my vision, I felt like the last thing I wanted to do was talk to anyone. But that's not true. I knew I couldn't trust my feelings. For me, I didn't want to put anyone out of their way to check on me. That itself is a limiting belief. If Jesus Christ died for you and me, do you think we should lean on each other since we're all valuable in the eyes of God?

Do not let your circumstances crush you! If you are alive, you can still encourage, inspire, love, and serve someone else. It is an odd thing to know that a person can come out stronger on the other end of adversity. I was almost crushed by suffering and pain, but God had a different plan for me in my life. God also has a different plan for you. Just because pain is present does not mean that God is absent. Remember, Christ suffered and bled so that man can live with God forever. Jesus' life was the atonement needed to pay for our sins. I don't know about you, but giving up one's innocent life, being betrayed, beaten, and so much more sounds a lot like suffering and pain.

We must not try to "survive" pain with power from our strength. We must look to Christ with confidence. We must know that God's will is better than ours, no matter the outcome. Despite my many prayer requests for healing in my eyes, God has not healed my eyes with perfect 20/20 vision. Does God answer prayers? Yes. Did God answer my prayer for my will for my life? No. With our power, the pain will indeed crush us, our spirit, our family, and our purpose. Think about Jesus before He was crucified. Jesus Christ, both fully God and fully man, knew He would be betrayed, arrested, and crucified. In the middle of the night, He took three disciples with Him: Peter, James, and John. He simply asked them to pray. Jesus Christ asked human beings to pray!

Jesus doesn't "need" people, but yet He asked His creation to pray with Him. There was a slight problem. It was late at night. Jesus, knowing He would die soon, walked a short distance away way from the disciples and began to pray.

Christ wept and prayed to God because of the upcoming pain and brutal suffering He would soon endure. Jesus knew how to speak to the Father. Unfortunately, when He went back to the disciples, they were doing what you and I would probably be doing in the middle of the night, sleeping. Yep, the three closest people to Jesus, the Son of God, were sleeping when He asked for their help. I cannot judge them because I most likely would have done the same thing. I'm going to share what the Bible says so you can read it. Pay close attention to Jesus and His disciples. Take note of the pain that is about to happen. Lastly, see that Jesus did not let the lack of support from His friends crush Him. He kept going and reached out to them more than they reached out to Him. Here's what the Bible says:

"36 Then Jesus came with them to a place called Gethsemane, and said to the disciples, "Sit here while I go and pray over there." 37 And He took with Him Peter and the two sons of Zebedee, and He began to be sorrowful and deeply distressed. 38 Then He said to them, "My soul is exceedingly sorrowful, even to death. Stay here and watch with Me." 39 He went a little farther and fell on His face, and prayed, saying, "O My Father, if it is possible, let this cup pass from Me; nevertheless, not as I will, but as You will." 40 Then He came to the disciples and found them sleeping, and said to Peter, "What! Could you not watch with Me one hour? 41 Watch and pray, lest you enter into temptation. The spirit indeed is willing, but the flesh is weak." 42 Again, a second time, He went away and prayed, saying, "O My Father, if this cup cannot pass away from Me unless I drink it, Your will be done." 43 And He came and found them asleep again, for their eyes were heavy. 44 So He left them, went away again, and prayed the third time, saying the same words. 45 Then He came to His disciples and said to them, "Are you still sleeping and resting? Behold, the hour is at hand, and the Son of Man is being betrayed into the hands of sinners. 46 Rise, let us be going. See, My betrayer is at hand."

Matthew 26:36-46 New King James Version (NKJV)

We mess up all the time. We'll continue to mess up because we're not Jesus. This part of Jesus' life is excruciating for me to read. Every time I think about how we as humans left Christ alone, I feel embarrassed and shameful. Thank God for His grace, mercy, and forgiveness! Though Christ was about to endure pain and suffering, He reached out to others and God the Father. My point is we need to reach out to loved ones when we're hurting, but we can't place our "faith" in them. Why? Because we're people. Jesus didn't ask Peter, James, and John to run a marathon with their legs tied together through an obstacle course while blindfolded. He asked them to pray. However, tiredness and fatigue overpowered their desire to support and encourage. So, we must ask others for support and love even though they may fail.

We must also run to the Father who has His arms open. The one true God who is and who will always be. God is faithful. God does answer prayers according to His will. Jesus knew this and affirmed this in verse 42 by saying, "O My Father, if this cup cannot pass away from Me unless I drink it, Your will be done'" (Matt. 26:42). This is a complicated truth for some people.

Unfortunately, some people choose not to believe in God because of this truth. The truth is God answers prayers His way and not yours. Again, we do not pray for God to do our will. We pray for God to do His perfect will. Jesus prayed if this cup, the upcoming pain, and suffering, could pass then let it pass. The crucial part of Christ's prayer is "Your will be done."

So just because you pray for healing and healing does not happen, it does not mean God doesn't care. Nor does it mean God is unable to heal. It means that God's will is different from your will. Sometimes, we may "disagree" with God's will. Someone did not get better and died. Maybe someone didn't get that job they desperately needed and prayed for. Too many times, when our prayers are not answered how we want them, we place doubt in the gap between God and us. Instead of putting doubt in the difference, we need to fill that gap with trust. I heard a pastor speak about this concept.

If our prayers aren't answered and we place doubt in the gap, we're setting ourselves up to be crushed mentally, physically, emotionally, and spiritually. All of it matters. Doubting is easy. It doesn't take energy to doubt, but it takes energy to trust. Trust requires us to let go of control and place someone in front of us. We cannot let doubt crush us. Though the pain is there, we can still trust God. Even though the prayer wasn't answered the way we wanted, we can always trust God. Also, when our friends fall asleep when we need them the most, we can still love our friends and trust God.

Application

When dealing with pain and suffering, reach out to loved ones for support.

When dealing with pain and suffering, reach out to God.

When someone needs your help, try not to fall asleep when they genuinely need your help.

Take some time to reflect on this chapter. Afterward, share your thoughts on social media using the hashtag "#PainFormation".

6. TAKE CARE OF YOURSELF

Time is an interesting thing because it's always "ticking." Day after day, we get older. You don't wake in the morning and say, "Well, I can't wait to deal with some pain today! Yay!" If you do, then stay away from me. Honestly, each time I've dealt with pain, I was not expecting it. Pain can come in times of happiness like when I was walking around Disney before my whole gallbladder incident. Believe me, I wouldn't have forked all that money out for a vacation if I knew I'd end up in the ambulance. It just happened. We don't "plan" for pain, and I am not saying to plan for depression. That would be a little weird. What I am saying is take care of yourself and stop wasting time.

Time is the most valuable asset you have. No matter when you read this book, yesterday is gone.

There's nothing you can do about it. The choices you made yesterday are in the history books. Each daily choice becomes a habit. Those habits become your behavior. Some patterns are better than others. What you have to be careful of is waiting to pursue your dreams and passions. Sickness can come at any time. Tomorrow is not promised to anyone. So, it doesn't have to be an illness that results in death.

My goal is not to be morbid and creepy by talking about death. I'm a realist. You have one life on Earth. Stop putting off things that you want to do. Take care of yourself. Study your Bible. Pray daily to God. Disciple others. Get involved at your church. Pursue your passions. Make your family a priority.

The Phone Call

It was a Monday night. I had a sinus infection, and I had asked Alison to pick up the prescription. Well, I also have a sweet tooth, so I asked her to stop by the grocery store and get me some treats. Our son was with me at the house. Alison left, and I was wrestling Eli. About 25 minutes passed when my phone rang. Alison was calling, asking what I wanted from the store and I told her. Afterward, we said goodbye and that we loved each other. Ten minutes passed, and she called me again. I thought she had another question, but I was wrong. She was sobbing, and it was tough to understand what she was saying. She had just been in a car accident. She wasn't hurt, but she was freaked out.

The car she was driving had the car seat in it, and I had Eli with me at the house. Yea, that was fun. A church member and her daughter came and watched Eli. Thank God! On my way to pick up Alison, I started thanking God that Alison was still alive. I began to replay all the things we "talked" about doing but never did. We talked about making a lot of intentional family memories. But they were just that, "talk." Sure, we have a date night every Friday, but we had not done the things we just merely talked about. I began to question why haven't we done those things. I realized we didn't plan and follow through. Time is not going to wait for us to make a plan with our family. I took that painful situation of my wife's possible death to make an empowering decision. I went from "Yea, we should do this or that" to "While, I'm alive, I will be more intentional with time with my family."

A few weeks ago, I surprised Alison with a five-day trip to Disney World in Florida. This will be the first time that Alison, Eli, and I will go on vacation all by ourselves. We're not visiting family or going to a church event. We're unplugging and spending time together. I'm not saying that life is about family trips. I am saying take care of your family in the way that works for you all. Just don't have any regrets with the time you have. Once that time is gone, it's gone. There is no rewind button. Make it count. Do the things you want to do. Learn that skill you've always wanted to learn. Be careful of ending a conversation on a wrong note. Who knows, it might be the last time you may see each other.

I'm sure you've heard people say, "Take care of yourself so you can take care of others." They usually talk about the flight attendant telling you to put the oxygen mask over your face first before you try to help someone else. We've heard it time and time again. Think about it. The things that are in our control should give us peace when we control them. Some situations are way out of our reach. However, there are some things that we do control that could keep us from growing in life.

In one year, I had two root canals....yea! I didn't learn after my first one. I am in control of my dental health. Once again, I may brush and floss my teeth every night, and yet I might still have a tooth issue. Nevertheless, I did something to help try to prevent a problem. To not try at all would be a waste.

Someone might say, "We're all going to die anyway. So, what's the point of living?" Well, even amid pain, there is joy and peace. The love that we get to experience from God and others is a blessing. When I was lying in a dentist chair, and he began drilling in my mouth the second time, I became sad. There I was, dealing with a health issue that I had given little effort to improve from last time.

Your health definitely may not be a tooth issue. At the same time, get yourself together. Too many people are relying on you. Whether it's your kids, spouse, friends, coworkers, they're counting on you. There are people who you haven't even met who will benefit and grow from knowing you, but you won't be able to help them if your oxygen mask isn't on first.

Take Care of Yourself Checklist

This list is in no way foolproof. It is geared towards helping you reflect on your current habits and direction in life.

Time
In the last month, what have you spent most of your time doing?

Remember, we make time for what we want to do.

Money
In the last month, other than bills, what have you spent most of your money on?

Remember, our money follows our heart.

Family
In the last month, do you wish you spent more quality time with your family?

Remember, there's nothing wrong with having expensive things. Just don't forget that a luxury car or big house won't come and visit you in the hospital. They'll rust and fall apart.

Spiritual
In the last month, did you make an effort to grow daily with Jesus?

Vocational
In the last month, have you been pursuing excellence in your job?

Purpose
In the last month, what are some dreams about your life that you've had?

Share how you did on the checklist on social media using the hashtag "#PainFormation"

7. DECISIONS, DECISIONS

I'm a problem solver. I'm a fixer. If I don't know the answer to your question or problem, I'll find someone who does. Call me weird, but I like to be under pressure. At work, I don't mind pressure. It is not the craziness part where everyone is running around like a chicken with its head out off. I look past the confusion and craziness and focus on the solution or peace that may come from facing the situation.

Naturally, I'm a decider. There are times when I don't want to make a single decision. Usually, that's after church on Sundays since I'm a pastor. During service, I'll make so many decisions in a few hours that I become "decision fatigued." Alison could ask me if I wanted chocolate-covered soap for lunch and I'd probably agree. I share that to be honest and say I'm not superman. Everyone has their strengths and weaknesses.

Whether you like to or not, decisions must be made. It's funny to think about it because some decisions are easy, but we make them difficult. Like the complicated questions such as, "What do you want to eat?" or "What should I wear today?" Sometimes we make things way more complicated than needed.

Unfortunately, that energy wasted on simple decisions burns us so when the time comes for an empowering decision, we throw in the towel. Claiming an empowering decision takes focus, faith, and energy. Yes, the obstacle may still be present, but when we can "wrestle" with our doubt and win, amazing things can happen.

Here's the thing, in order to wrestle our fears and doubts, we must acknowledge they are there. Too often, people avoid success and accomplishment due to fear. From my experience, fear can and will paralyze you. Fear and doubt take no prisoners. They are like the yin and yang of ruining lives. Fear creeps in and makes you a little boy at night in his room, wanting mommy to turn on his nightlight. I know. When I was a kid, I watched Child's Play. Yea, the movie with the killer doll named Chucky. Don't judge me. Well, don't judge my mom. After I saw that movie, I was scared to death. I could not sleep alone in my room. I slept in the same room and bed as my older sister for quite some time! Sorry, Von.

The darkness would consume me. I feared for my life. The only way I could even sleep was to know that someone was right beside me. The nightlight was no good for me. I needed another person just in case Chucky came so I could leave my sister to deal with him. Sorry again Von. Looking back, it seems silly. How could I be so afraid that a child's doll would come alive and kill me in real life? Sure, I was a child, but my perception became my reality. I was so fearful of something that would never happen that I changed my behavior to suit my fear.

Even as adults, we do the same thing. We become consumed by the darkness of fear. Some things are genuinely fearful events that may occur. However, more than often, we're afraid of the "doll" that's going to come and kill us. Even when I started writing this book, it took a little while to start sharing that I'm writing a book. I had to take a step back and tell myself to keep going. I would tell people I was writing a book and they would say, "Oh cool. On what?" That was my moment to stare fear and doubt in the face. Fear that they would reject me and doubt that they wouldn't be interested.

Fear and doubt still pop up in my life now and then. This book is not about "deleting" fear and uncertainty. If I told you that, I'd be lying to you because I still deal with it. What I can tell you is when fear and doubt come alive in my mind and heart, I stop everything. It's hard to explain. It's like those cloudy, rainy mornings when you wake up and want to stay in bed but need to get up for work or take care of your kids. You know what you want to do, which is to do nothing. You also understand what you need to do, which is to get up and fulfill your responsibilities. To me, it's as simple as making a choice. So, after noticing fear and doubt, I choose to move forward, no matter the consequences. I have been consumed by fear and uncertainty. But a great friend of mine, Clayton, gave me a book. This book, 20,000 Days, changed my perspective on time.

Let me tell you; you can die at any moment. I'm not morbid. It's true, like it or not. When I see it from that perspective, I'm no longer fearful and doubtful about the situation. It makes me laugh. When put in perspective, we gain a broader picture of what truly matters. We are called to do God's will on Earth. There's no time to let fear and doubt get in the way of our ticking clock of life. When it's all said and done, no one will say, "James almost lived his life to the fullest.

Too bad fear and doubt trapped him." Fear and doubt can be defeated, not by my power, but through the power of Christ. Jesus died for me. I'm pretty valuable, and you are too. When someone pays for your sins and places their life for yours, you have to make it count. Jesus did not die for you to be fearful and doubtful. Sure, moments come, and they have to be dealt with. But you cannot be "taken out" by feelings. Don't trust your feelings because they're iffy. I repeat DO NOT Trust Your Feelings. You can embrace your feelings without making them your reality. You need to trust God. You can also ask for help from loved ones or even take a day off of work to rest.

Be ready for the two monsters who are coming to kill your dreams and goals. Fear and doubt are lurking around ready to pounce on your life and swipe your feet right from under you. Make the decision that your life will count. Each day is a blessing. You may feel fear, but it doesn't have to be your reality. You may feel like the doll is coming to kill you at night, but help comes to those who ask.

Where Are You Going?

A great question to ask is, "Where am I going?" No, I don't mean that you're going on a vacation. Life is a journey with many ups and downs. Some seasons are better than others. Sometimes life feels like you can't catch a break because it is filled with hurt. Even though we experience pain, we can still be on a journey in life heading somewhere. Again, the question comes to "Where are you going?" What do you want out of this life? What does "Success" mean to you? What's the best impact you can make on others while you're alive? When you die, what will be said about you? It's not so easy to pinpoint all of those answers, but it's better to be moving in the direction of the desired outcome than not. It's like writing this book. I've always wanted to write one. I started with a plan to finish. However, tomorrow is not promised to me. So, I may die before I finish this book, or I may not. Either way, I will continue to work on it day by day until it's finished.

Keeping the end in mind comes by determining where you are going, and despite the struggle, you will do your best to get there. If you planned a trip to Disney and got a flat tire on the way there, I'm sure you'd fix that flat and keep going. Let's say you planned a trip to Disney, but a family emergency came up. You would most likely leave Disney in the rearview mirror for family and loved ones. So, keeping the end in mind is not final, but it helps us use our time more wisely. So, with pain and suffering happening in our lives, how can we keep moving forward?

The other day my head was aching so bad I could barely move. I was in bed by 7:00 pm curled up in pain. I took all the medicine I could. I was not writing, working, spending quality time with family, laughing, or playing. I was hurting and wanted it to go away. For hours, I laid in bed with the feeling of a drill going in my skull. While I was in pain, I reflected throughout the day on what my decisions were before I started to experience that pain. I woke up early, did my Bible study and prayed. I cleaned the house while Alison was at work. I planned my ideal week on how I'll spend my time at work and home. I accomplished my priorities for that day. Realizing that, I was at peace. Though I was very much in pain, I knew I didn't waste my time by sitting and watching tv all day. There's nothing wrong with that.

Just remember, time sitting and watching tv could be used to do other things even during commercials. My decisions for that day didn't just pop up. I didn't wake up saying, "Yep! I'm going to clean and finish my goals on my day off." Nope! I made a plan the week prior because I have been evaluating my time at home. Alison has been a stay at home mom for two years. She was temporarily working full-time for just a few months. So, I wanted to make sure I was helping out around the house even more since both of us have been working. I scheduled time during my off days to clean the house. This goes to keeping the end in mind. I want to and will be known as a husband who loved his wife publicly and privately. Alison is huge on Acts of Service. So, I am showing her love in her language. When we're not intentional about our time and life, we drift through time.

Not every minute of your life needs to be planned. At the same time, when you lay your head down to sleep and think about the day, you never want to have regrets due to precious time wasted. In the words of Christian Rapper KB, "I have wasted so many years. I can't rewind." If you are having trouble figuring out what's your end in mind, you need to work on that right now. Spend some time in prayer, read the life of Christ, ask God for a vision for your life.

My end in mind is simple: be a Christ-follower, make disciples, love my wife each day, be a godly father, use each gift that God has blessed me with, don't waste my life.

For you, it may be something completely different. Mine is simple, but yet powerful truths that help me on my journey. Even though I'm blind in one eye with a rare hereditary eye disease, I will use the gifts God has blessed me with. Even though I have scars all over my body from psoriasis, I will make disciples. Even though my parents divorced when I was a child, I will love my wife each day and be a godly father to my children.

My pain does not have power over my faith in Christ and who He calls me to be. Christ overcame the world, so why would I try to do everything on my own?

Application

Where are you going?

What do you want out of this life?

What does "Success" mean to you?

What's the best impact you can make on others while you're alive?

When you die, what do you want others to say about you?

With pain and suffering happening in your life, how can you keep moving forward?

Now Get There One Goal at a Time

It is not my intention for this book to be cheesy nor overwhelming. Life is complicated but yet simple. I know, right? We know we should love people, however, get so angry at each other even over the smallest things. There have been times in my life when I wanted to throw in the towel. Not in a self-harming, run away from my family and start over way, but throw in the towel during different challenging situations that just seemed too hard. I wanted to quit. I wanted to take my ball and go home. We must not stop when things get tough. Instead, we must rely on God, ask for help and support from loved ones, and take it one goal at a time. Yes, one goal at a time.

If I'm fighting with my wife and we're both irate, yelling at each other, we should probably use self-control and take a step back. Waiting for another day down the road to resolve conflict isn't wrong, remember the next day isn't promised. So, a goal would be to signal that we need a break from each other for a few minutes to cool down. Could something happen in those few minutes that would be life-changing? Absolutely. The point is to accomplish unity sooner rather than later. Just like dealing with rejection, the sooner you confront those fears, the sooner you'll be able to move on with your life.

The goals must be established beforehand. If you don't have goals within your marriage, how can you both know that taking a break during an argument is even an option? If you don't set goals for who you want to be in life, then how will you know to take that rejection and face those fears and doubts with facts about yourself?

I have a goal to be a Christ-follower. For me, I am not going to sit on the sidelines. I'm going to serve and love others as Christ did. At the same time, with my eyes being the way they are, I get a lot of weird looks and questions about my eye. As a child and teenager, I took this so personally that I believed God made a mistake. Publicly, I was funny and made people laugh. Privately, I was broken. It wasn't until I made it a goal with the one life I have to be a Christ-follower no matter what. My circumstance would not disprove God's love for me.

8. TRUSTING GOD DURING PAIN

I remember it just like it was yesterday. Alison showed me the test, and it read pregnant. I was stunned and excited. We were having our second child. Eli was becoming a big brother. We hugged and kissed each other in excitement. We weren't trying to have another baby at that moment in time, but you know how things go. We sat down and started discussing our plan to keep it quiet and then share later with family and loved ones.

Some time had passed, and we were ready to call our families. We called and shared the great news. My mother and Alison's parents were excited for us. We then called Stephen and his wife Wendy who are also family. They shared in delight with us. It is hard keeping a secret. I mean, you want to blurt it out from on top of a mountain. If someone said, "Hey

James, how are you?" I just wanted to shout, "We're pregnant!" However, I kept it calm until we told our family. After our phone calls, we spent time together, kissed each other goodnight, and went to sleep.

A few days passed. I don't remember much of what would soon come to follow except that Alison was in the bathroom for a very long time. She told me she was bleeding a lot and she thought we had lost the baby. I wasn't sure what to say or do. This was not the time for me to pretend to be big and strong. This was the time for comfort and love. We hugged each other and started calling to schedule an appointment. This turned out to be even more devastating because Alison was a stay at home mom. We had three people in our home with one income.

I had Blue Cross Blue Shield insurance through my job. Unfortunately, neither Alison or Eli was covered in my plan. The problem was that the only place that accepted her insurance was a local doctor who lost his license. That's it. We did not know if we lost the baby and couldn't afford anywhere that didn't take her insurance. It was hell. I was angry and sad. I was confused and lost. There I was, working a full-time job in ministry and still couldn't afford insurance that would have been accepted to get us an appointment right away. The whole time this was going on, I was asking God to help us, to give us peace, comfort, wisdom, and strength. The fear was crumbling my mind. Could God hear my prayers? Why did God allow this to happen?

I couldn't stop thinking about the pain because it distracted me from feeling the pain. We had to wait for days before we got an appointment. Waiting for answers was excruciating. We cried for days as our appointment approached. While we were in the waiting room, we talked, laughed, and played with Eli. It was like we both secretly already knew what the doctor would say. Finally, we were called back. Not long after the tests, the results were final. We were no longer pregnant. We had lost the baby. The doctor left the room, and we sat there in silence and disbelief. Our joy of life had been replaced with the grief of death. The smiles were gone. There were no laughs. Just pain. Unfiltered pain to the core of our souls.

Even now, thinking about it makes me wonder who he or she would have been on earth. I have faith that God's will was done and that I will see him or her in Heaven. After the news, I told Alison we should go out to eat. It was time to be together as a family. Later that night, we called our family and friends and gave them the news. They were all comforting to us.

Thank God for His people.

Even in my darkest hour, I had to trust in God. I had an event coming up. Some churches celebrate babies with families by doing a baby dedication or child dedication. They want parents to celebrate the new addition to their family. I've seen it done many times and in different ways. I've done it is as a part of Sunday morning service by the pastor inviting the families up to dedicate their babies, I've said a word of encouragement and prayer. I've also done it as a standalone service with a short sermon.

My message would typically be about how God desires for us to be loving parents and for us to reflect the love that He gives us towards our children. I'd share some Bible verses, and about how when my son Eli was born, it was one of the best days of my life. After the message, I'd pray for the child, the parents, and the church. This prayer is a three-step process and is very important because it encompasses all parties involved. I want to cover the child in prayer, but also to pray for the parents for the steep road ahead. Lastly, I want to engage everyone in the room, to focus on giving, caring, and showing love for the families.

Although I've done a baby dedication many times before and enjoyed it, this upcoming was different. We had just gotten the news about the miscarriage on Friday and the baby dedication service was on Sunday. I was struggling and could not see how I could teach families that God desires for us to be godly parents and how God loves children when we had just lost our baby. I couldn't believe God was doing this to me. God knew I was going to lead a baby dedication to numerous families after I lost my baby.

Honestly, I considered quitting. I was hurting beyond belief. On the other end of that, it almost felt as if it was a necessity to share the message of God's love even while I was hurting. I had to make sure that my circumstance didn't come as a fact against our loving God. In other words, if God loves babies, why did we have a miscarriage and lose our baby? Does this mean that God does not love babies? Of course not, but the thought did creep in my mind. That's why we have to be careful of our thoughts through the pain.

We can't trust ourselves when we are hurting. We have to rely on faith, friends, and facts. I knew that I could depend on God's love to lead me through the baby dedication to celebrate the life of a child. I knew then that it wasn't through my power that I would be able to do this but through the power of God and faith.

When the day arrived, and as families came in smiling and laughing with each other, the clock began giving me the five-minute countdown. As time was ticking and I was meeting parents, grandparents, siblings, and the babies, I was just so thankful. I was grateful to God for His faithfulness. I was grateful to God that I was alive, healthy, and married to a beautiful woman. I was thankful that I had a healthy baby boy at home. I was thankful that I could stand there on stage on my own two feet. I was grateful for my vision and that God restored it numerous times. As I stood there and thought about all these blessings, I realized all the promises God has made to me. God's promise is sure. I also realized that just because I asked for something does not mean that it's in the will of God.

As I said before, I would rather be in the will of God than in the will of James. When I finished the baby dedication message that day, I felt a peace come over me. I believe that God used that hurt to encourage and strengthen and share the word of God's love for countless families in that room. That was painful, yet through the power of Christ, I overcame that doubt. Even though sometimes I still think about my child, I'm always thankful for the opportunity that God has given me.

Life-Long Journey

Pain Formation is also not about ignoring the problem. It's about dealing with the pain and suffering with the love of friends, family, and God. When you're by yourself, it is a whole lot easier for a robber to do you harm because there's no one around you to protect you. If they take you out, then they'll be able to take what you have and leave you in a pool of suffering.

Pain is the same thing as a robber because you're the victim who ends up hurt. It's not looking to comfort you. Pain is not looking to help you go to sleep at night. Pain and suffering are two of the most disturbing things in our lives. They can drive us to self-harm, doubt, worry, stress, illness, depression, separation, divorce, and anxiety. The list goes on. The point of Pain Formation is to know that you will witness pain and suffering in your life. It is not unusual for people to deal with pain and suffering. If you take time and look around yourself, you will see that other people are in pain and are suffering. You cannot do this alone. You will not do this alone. You will get help.

When pain comes, sometimes it goes away quickly and sometimes it stays for a while. There are benefits to being proactive. We can do our best to try and have everything in perfect order. I completely understand. It's like getting healthy because you don't want to become sick. At the same time, you can still become sick. Then what? I've shared stories about how reactive I have been when dealing with pain and suffering. Because at the end of the day, it hurts. The pain comes. You have to feel it. You have to embrace it. The most crucial part of my final comments is that you have to move forward. I could sit home alone, complaining that I'm blind in one eye because of a rare hereditary disease. I could sit at home and cover up my body with long sleeve shirts and jeans because of my psoriasis. I could abandon my family because of the lack of fatherhood that I've had in my life. I could quit my job and give up on my aspirations and dreams because I flunked out of college. There are many things that I could do. However, there are better things that I will do.

This book is not a happy go lucky read one-time book. My life story through years of pain and suffering is hard to share. I have gone through years of doubt, hurt, and wondering why me. I highly encourage you to read this book more than one time. Give some copies out to your colleagues, friends, and family. Share the message. Believe it and apply it to your life. I also will ask you to read this book maybe once a year or at least remember where it is on your bookshelf.

Keep this book. Because when pain comes, you'll have my stories of stress, doubt, and fear from my pain and suffering.

You are going to make it. You are going to do amazing things. You are successful. If you're reading this, you're alive, and when you're alive, there's still time to do great things. When you still have time to do great things, you can make a difference. When you make a difference, you honor the life that God has given you.

May God bless you in your journey of life. No matter where it takes you. No matter what sickness, illness, or harm may come, don't worry. The pain will happen, but you can keep going. You will keep going. Remember, there is no one else on earth like you. There is no one else on earth that has the same story as you. People are relying on you, and you will fulfill your purpose. I look forward to meeting you and hearing how you've persevered through the pain in your life.

ACKNOWLEDGMENTS

I want to thank my wife, Alison. You sacrifice so much for me. I am truly honored to be your husband. Your love for me can be seen throughout this book. I am thankful that God brought us together. I love you.

Mom & Von,
It's a blessing to have you as family. I couldn't ask for a better mother and sister. God used our hurt in Statesville to bring us closer than ever.

Stephen & Wendy,
I can't imagine where I'd be without your love, support, and guidance. Thank you for helping me when I needed it the most. I'm thankful you're a part of my family.

Mike & Kristen,
Thank you for helping us through a difficult season. We love you guys!

Thanks to Darrin & Kelly, David & Lisa, Joyce, Clayton, Camron, Jason & Rachel, and many more!

Enjoy this book? Stay up to date with me via my blog at TheLifeofWilson.com

THE LIFE OF WILSON

Connect with me here:
Facebook: James2theWilson
Instagram: James2theWilson
Twitter: James2theWilson

Join Our Community:
Facebook.com/groups/PainFormation

For speaking engagements, email:
James@thelifeofwilson.com

www.ingramcontent.com/pod-product-compliance
Lightning Source LLC
LaVergne TN
LVHW050934080826
845145LV00004B/1253

9780578498515